About the Author™

Meet

Laurence Yep

Alice B. McGinty

The Rosen Publishing Group's
PowerKids Press™
New York

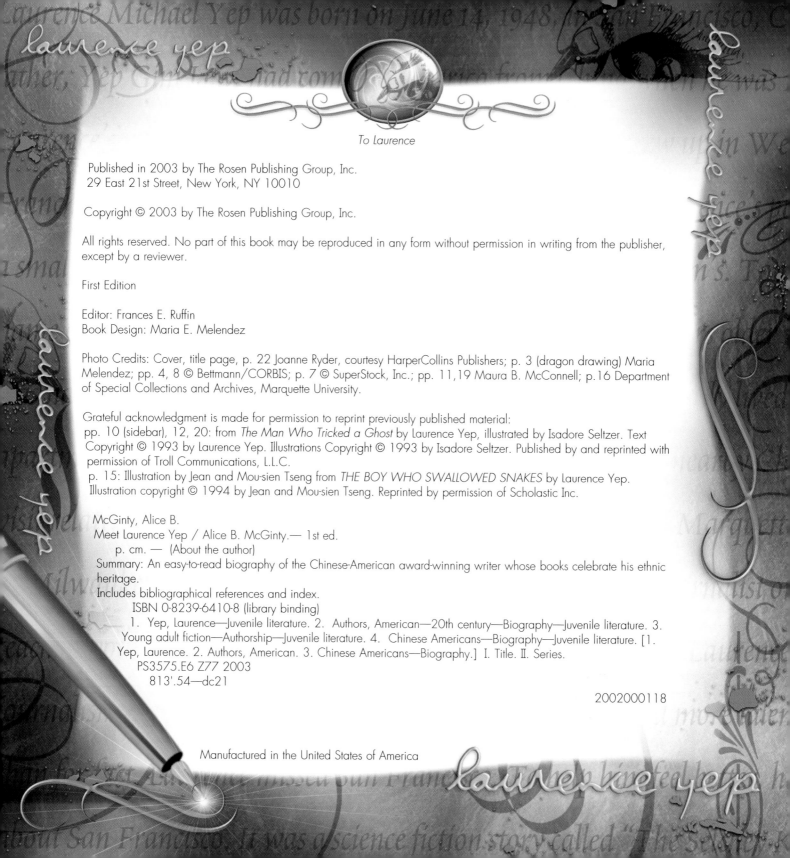

To Laurence

Published in 2003 by The Rosen Publishing Group, Inc.
29 East 21st Street, New York, NY 10010

First Edition

Editor: Frances E. Ruffin
Book Design: Maria E. Melendez

Photo Credits: Cover, title page, p. 22 Joanne Ryder, courtesy HarperCollins Publishers; p. 3 (dragon drawing) Maria Melendez; pp. 4, 8 © Bettmann/CORBIS; p. 7 © SuperStock, Inc.; pp. 11,19 Maura B. McConnell; p.16 Department of Special Collections and Archives, Marquette University.

Grateful acknowledgment is made for permission to reprint previously published material:
pp. 10 (sidebar), 12, 20: from *The Man Who Tricked a Ghost* by Laurence Yep, illustrated by Isadore Seltzer. Text Copyright © 1993 by Laurence Yep. Illustrations Copyright © 1993 by Isadore Seltzer. Published by and reprinted with permission of Troll Communications, L.L.C.
p. 15: Illustration by Jean and Mou-sien Tseng from *THE BOY WHO SWALLOWED SNAKES* by Laurence Yep. Illustration copyright © 1994 by Jean and Mou-sien Tseng. Reprinted by permission of Scholastic Inc.

McGinty, Alice B.
  Meet Laurence Yep / Alice B. McGinty.— 1st ed.
    p. cm. — (About the author)
  Summary: An easy-to-read biography of the Chinese-American award-winning writer whose books celebrate his ethnic heritage.
  Includes bibliographical references and index.
    ISBN 0-8239-6410-8 (library binding)
    1. Yep, Laurence—Juvenile literature. 2. Authors, American—20th century—Biography—Juvenile literature. 3. Young adult fiction—Authorship—Juvenile literature. 4. Chinese Americans—Biography—Juvenile literature. [1. Yep, Laurence. 2. Authors, American. 3. Chinese Americans—Biography.] I. Title. II. Series.
    PS3575.E6 Z77 2003
      813'.54—dc21

                                                                    2002000118

Manufactured in the United States of America

Contents

1 Finding a Balance 5

2 Laurence's Family 6

3 The Daily Routine 9

4 A Place in the World 10

5 Chinatown 13

6 In High School 14

7 Becoming a Writer 17

8 *Sweetwater* 18

9 A Writer's Life 21

10 In His Own Words 22

Glossary 23

Index 24

Web Sites 24

Finding a Balance

As a child, Laurence Yep simply wanted to be an American. Yet growing up in San Francisco, California, he was not accepted as one. People who were not Chinese only saw him as Chinese. To the Chinese, however, English-speaking Laurence Yep was too American.

Growing up, Laurence spent his life learning to balance being both Chinese and American. Though he lives proudly as an American, Laurence now understands and treasures his Chinese **heritage**. In his books, Laurence brings Chinese and Chinese American **cultures** to life. His stories and the story of his life will speak to all of us who struggle to know exactly who we are.

◀ *This photo of San Francisco's Chinatown was taken when Laurence was a young boy.*

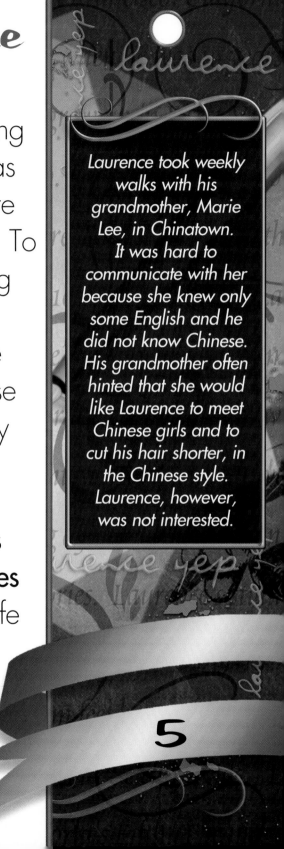

Laurence took weekly walks with his grandmother, Marie Lee, in Chinatown. It was hard to communicate with her because she knew only some English and he did not know Chinese. His grandmother often hinted that she would like Laurence to meet Chinese girls and to cut his hair shorter, in the Chinese style. Laurence, however, was not interested.

Laurence's Family

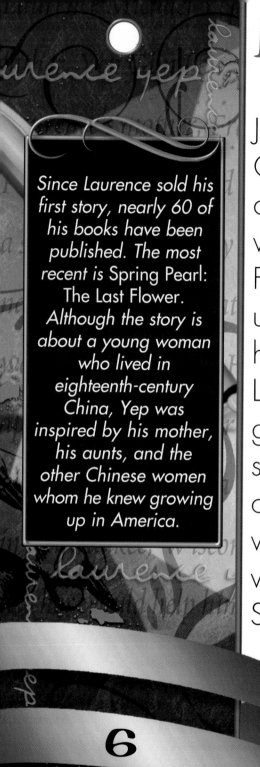

Since Laurence sold his first story, nearly 60 of his books have been published. The most recent is Spring Pearl: The Last Flower. Although the story is about a young woman who lived in eighteenth-century China, Yep was inspired by his mother, his aunts, and the other Chinese women whom he knew growing up in America.

Laurence Michael Yep was born on June 14, 1948, in San Francisco, California. His father, Yep Gim Lew, had come to America from China when he was 10 years old. Laurence's mother, Franche Lee, was born in Ohio and grew up in West Virginia. Franche's parents had come to America from China, too. Laurence's parents owned a small corner grocery store. The neighbors called the store Tom's. Tom was the American name of Laurence's father. Laurence's brother, who was 10 years older than Laurence, was named Thomas. His nickname was Spike. Laurence's family lived in a small apartment above their store. They often took the **cable car** to nearby **Chinatown** to visit relatives.

This photo of a cable car was taken in the 1950s. Cable cars still travel in the streets of San Francisco. ▶

Laurence yep

Laurence M...el...o was born on June 14, 1948, in San Francisco, Cali...

...came to America from...when he was 10

GRACE BALL SECRETARIAL COLLEGE

POWELL & MASON STS.

502

Now DANCING in the Orchid Room HOTEL ST. FRANCIS

POWELL AND MARKET

FISHERMENS WHARF 3 BLOCKS FROM TERMINAL

BAY AND TAYLOR

MUNICIPAL RAILWAY OF SAN FRANCISCO

...San Francisco. It was a science fiction story called The Selchey K...

Laurence Michael Yep was born on June 14, 1948, in San Francisco,

father, Yep Gim Lew had come to America from

about San Francisco. It was a science fiction story called "The Sel

The Daily Routine

Running the grocery store kept Laurence's family busy. His parents worked 12 hours every day. Laurence had many chores in the store, too. He put drinks in the refrigerator and salt pork in the meat counter. He stacked boxes and cans of food. To get cereal boxes onto the top shelf, Laurence tossed the boxes up to his father, who stood on a ladder. His father said that this was good practice for Laurence's basketball shot. Laurence's father taught his sons **athletic** skills. His brother, Spike, was good at athletics. Laurence did not do well at sports. Instead, he liked to read. When his parents read a story to him, Laurence read one back to them.

◀ *This is a Chinese-owned grocery store, photographed in the 1940s.*

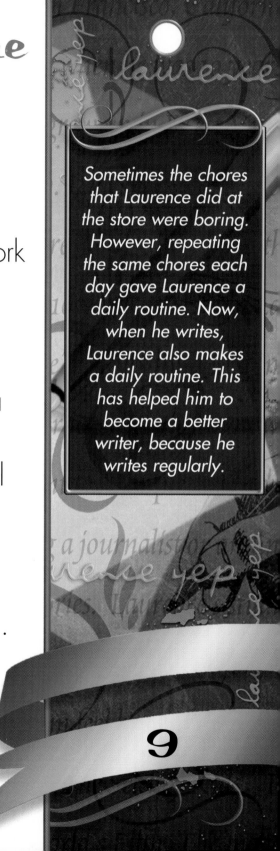

Sometimes the chores that Laurence did at the store were boring. However, repeating the same chores each day gave Laurence a daily routine. Now, when he writes, Laurence also makes a daily routine. This has helped him to become a better writer, because he writes regularly.

A Place in the World

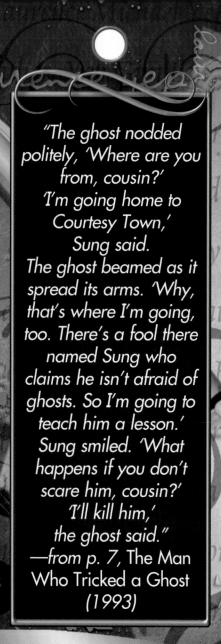

"The ghost nodded politely, 'Where are you from, cousin?'
'I'm going home to Courtesy Town,' Sung said.
The ghost beamed as it spread its arms. 'Why, that's where I'm going, too. There's a fool there named Sung who claims he isn't afraid of ghosts. So I'm going to teach him a lesson.'
Sung smiled. 'What happens if you don't scare him, cousin?'
'I'll kill him,' the ghost said."
—from p. 7, The Man Who Tricked a Ghost (1993)

Laurence's neighborhood housed a mix of families, including white, **Hispanic**, **Asian**, and African American families. When he was seven, the city tore down many of the homes and built low-income **housing projects**. Many of his friends moved away. As one of the only Asian American children, Laurence felt like an outsider. He had **asthma**, which made it difficult for him to breathe sometimes. When he had asthma attacks, Laurence's mother read to him while waiting for the doctor. One of Laurence's favorite books was *The Pirates of Oz*. Like Laurence, the **characters** in the book had to struggle to find their place in a new world.

Laurence sometimes writes about the Chinese legends, or stories, that his relatives told him. ▶

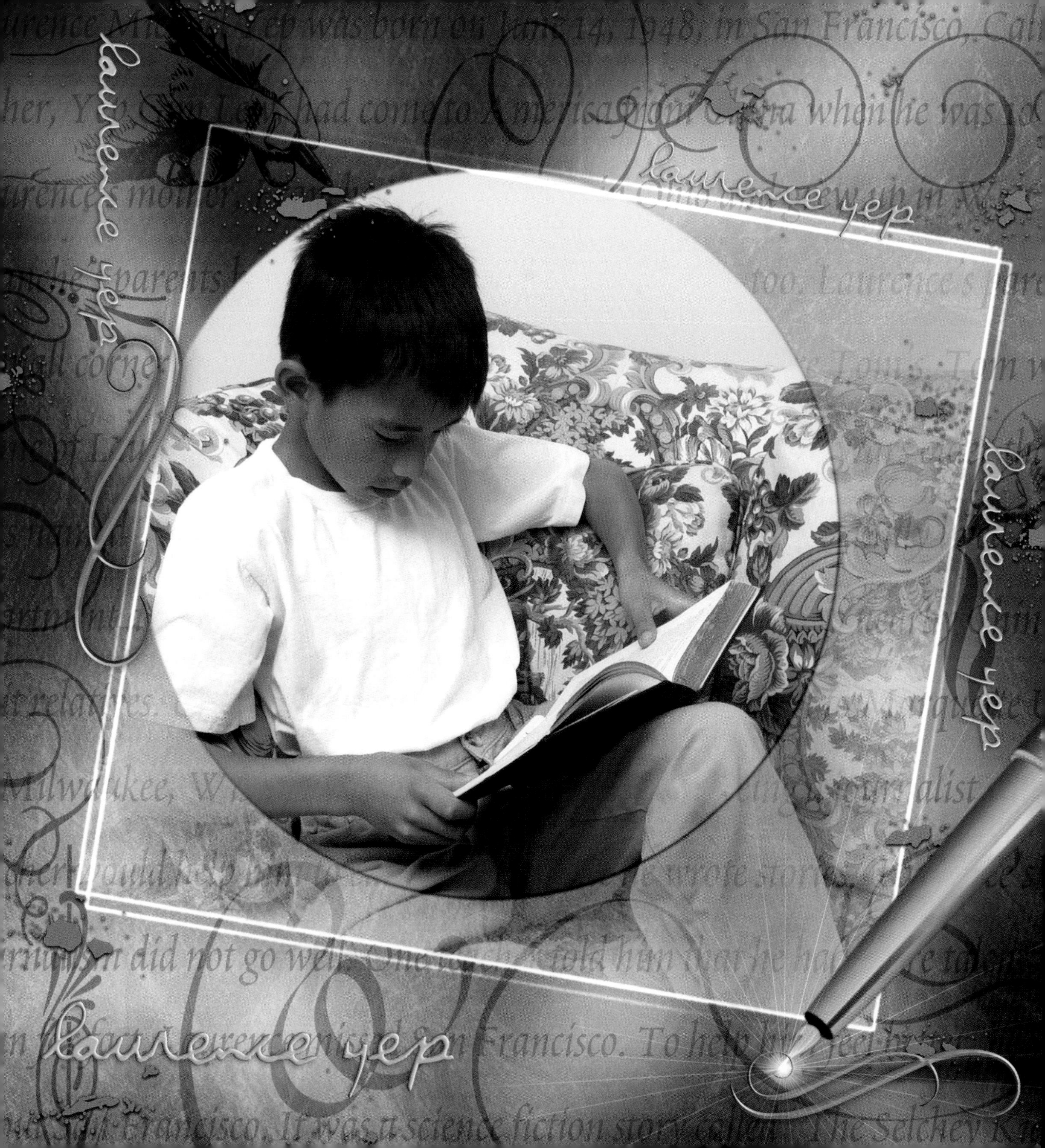
laurence yep
laurence yep
laurence yep
laurence yep

After another mile, the ghost announced it was Sung's turn and set him down on his feet. "Just how do you plan to scare Sung anyway?" he asked the ghost.

"Watch this!" The ghost's hair rose up in flaming spikes like twisted sword blades.

Sung, however, wasn't the least bit impressed. "I knew Sung quite well when I was alive. He'll just tell you to comb your hair."

"Wait. That's not all!" the ghost bragged. Its eyes started to glow a blood red and then it jerked off its head.

Sung merely yawned. "Since he can't afford candles, he might ask you to lend him your head as a lantern."

Chinatown

Laurence's struggles worsened when he went to school. He went to a **Catholic** school in Chinatown. Most of his schoolmates spoke both English and Chinese. At home Laurence's family spoke only English. Again, Laurence felt out of place. When his schoolmates told dirty jokes in Chinese so that their Catholic teachers wouldn't understand them, Laurence couldn't understand either. Although he was an *A* student, Laurence was put in a slower Chinese language class at school. Laurence **rebelled** against being Chinese American. He learned just enough Chinese to pass the class.

This is a page from Laurence's book ◀ The Man Who Tricked a Ghost, *published in 1993.*

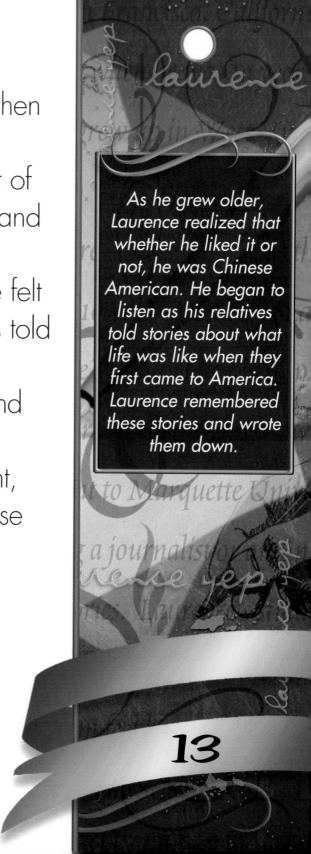

As he grew older, Laurence realized that whether he liked it or not, he was Chinese American. He began to listen as his relatives told stories about what life was like when they first came to America. Laurence remembered these stories and wrote them down.

In High School

Laurence was a good student at Saint Ignatius, a Catholic high school for boys. He was placed in the honors program. His favorite classes were in science. He and his friends enjoyed using an exploding paste that they discovered in chemistry class. Laurence decided to become a chemist when he grew up. Then, during his last year in high school, his English teacher, Father Becker, told Laurence and others that if they wanted an *A* in his class, they had to get a piece of writing accepted by a national magazine. Though all of them tried, nobody succeeded. Father Becker graded them fairly anyway, and Laurence discovered that he liked to write.

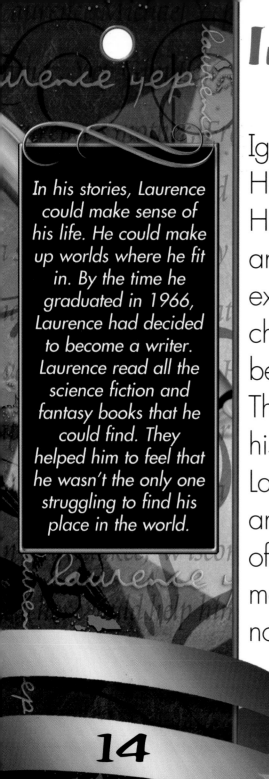

In his stories, Laurence could make sense of his life. He could make up worlds where he fit in. By the time he graduated in 1966, Laurence had decided to become a writer. Laurence read all the science fiction and fantasy books that he could find. They helped him to feel that he wasn't the only one struggling to find his place in the world.

Laurence's book The Boy Who Swallowed Snakes *is a story ▶ about a courageous boy.*

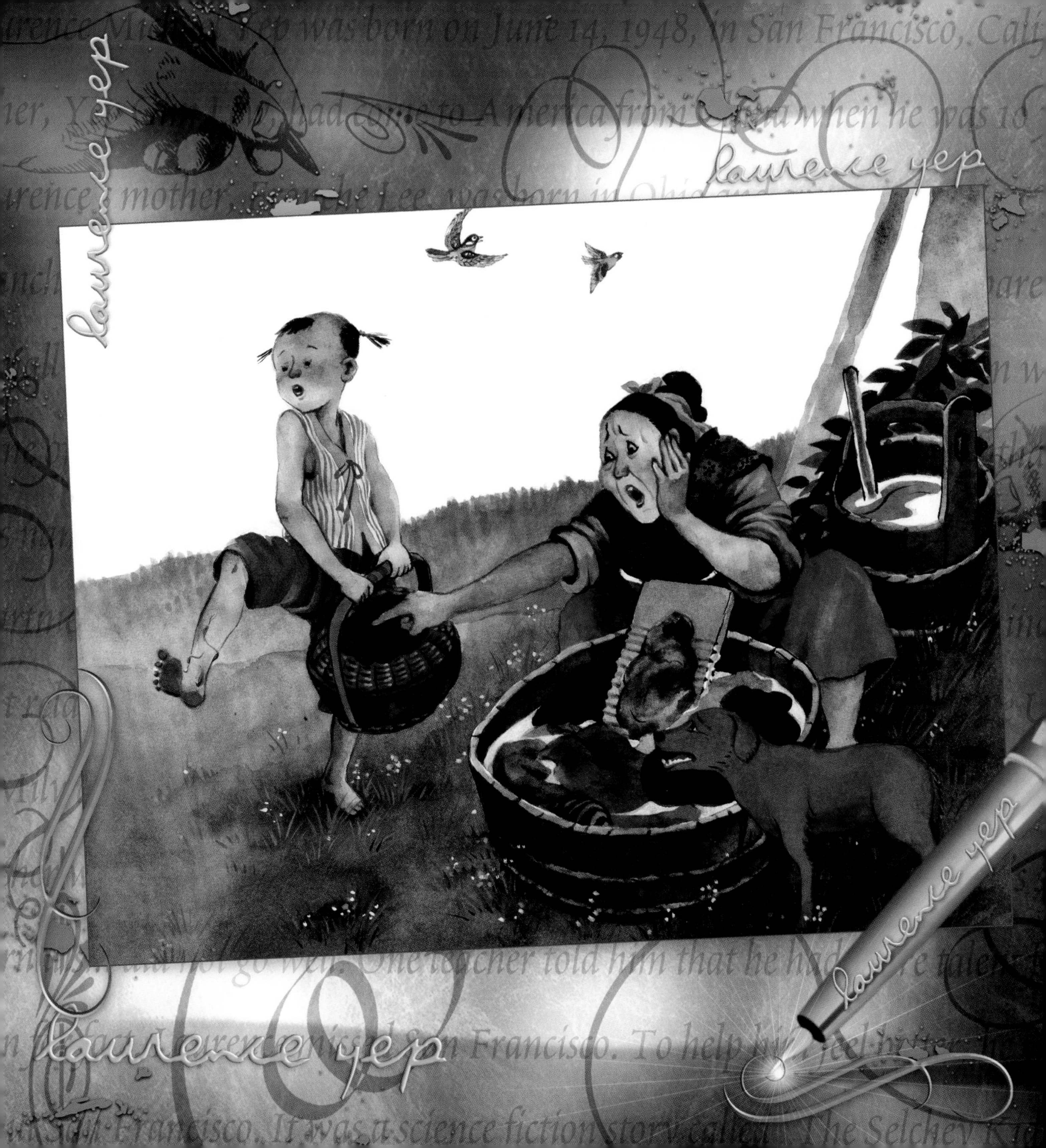
laurence yep

Becoming a Writer

Upon a teacher's suggestion, Laurence went to Marquette University in Milwaukee, Wisconsin. He studied **journalism**. Being a journalist or an English teacher would help him to earn money while he wrote stories. Laurence's studies in journalism did not go well. One teacher told him that he had more talent for **fiction** than for fact. Laurence missed San Francisco. To help himself feel better, he wrote a story about San Francisco. It was a science fiction story called "The Selchey Kids." Laurence sent it to one of his favorite science fiction magazines, *World's Fifth*. The magazine **published** his story!

◄ *Laurence studied journalism at Marquette University* (left) *and made many friends there.*

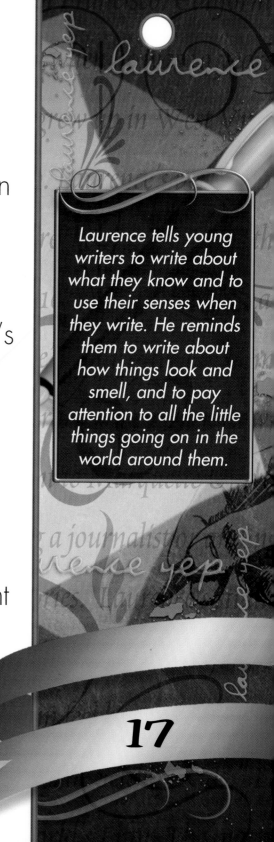

Laurence tells young writers to write about what they know and to use their senses when they write. He reminds them to write about how things look and smell, and to pay attention to all the little things going on in the world around them.

17

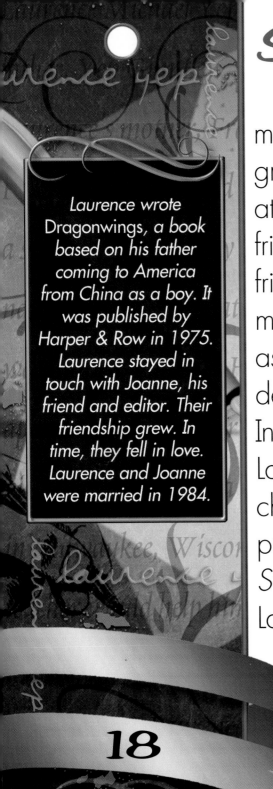

Sweetwater

Laurence left Marquette in 1968. He moved back West to finish college and graduate from the University of California at Santa Cruz. He kept in touch with his friends from Marquette, though. One good friend was Joanne Ryder, a student and a magazine **editor**. Joanne got a job as an assistant editor with the children's department of Harper & Row, Publishers, Inc. in New York City. She suggested that Laurence write a science fiction book for children. He did. In 1973, Harper & Row published Laurence's first book, called *Sweetwater*. Deciding to teach English, Laurence went to the State University of New York at Buffalo and earned a Ph.D. in English in 1975.

In his book Dragonwings, *Laurence based a character on his father, who liked to* ▶ *make and fly kites.*

laurence yep
laurence yep
laurence yep
laurence yep
Will Windrider take to the skies!
LAURENCE YEP
Dragonwings
GOLDEN MOUNTAIN CHRONICLES: 1903
25TH ANNIVERSARY EDITION

The Man Who Tricked a Ghost
BY LAURENCE YEP · PICTURES BY ISADORE SELTZER
laurence yep
laurence yep
laurence yep
laurence yep

A Writer's Life

Laurence and Joanne now live in Sunnyvale, California, close to San Francisco. Joanne writes children's books, too. Laurence teaches English part-time at the University of California. In his free time, he likes to take long walks. Since they live two blocks from the ocean, he and Joanne walk on the beach and watch sea otters and birds.

Laurence is one of few children's authors who writes about Chinese and Chinese American cultures. His books have won many awards. *Dragonwings* and *Dragon's Gate* both won Newbery Honor awards. Readers, both adults and children, like the way Laurence brings the worlds and the people in his stories to life.

◀ *Laurence's book* The Man Who Tricked a Ghost *is a story that takes place in China.*

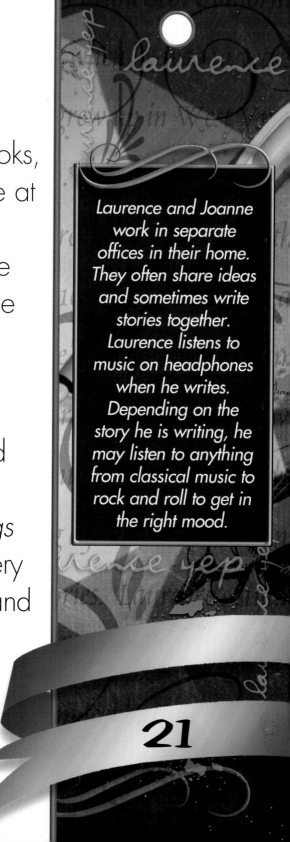

Laurence and Joanne work in separate offices in their home. They often share ideas and sometimes write stories together. Laurence listens to music on headphones when he writes. Depending on the story he is writing, he may listen to anything from classical music to rock and roll to get in the right mood.

21

In His Own Words

Laurence Yep

What life experiences do you draw on in your writing?

I grew up in an African American neighborhood where we ran a small corner grocery store, but I went to school every day in Chinatown. Mark Twain said that all his experiences on a riverboat gave him all the material he ever needed as a writer. I feel the same way about the people I met in both neighborhoods.

What's a typical working day like for you?

I work eight hours a day, six days a week. I spend about four hours in the morning writing and then another four hours answering letters or e-mails and doing research. Whenever I feel myself growing tired, I remind myself that my father used to work twelve hours a day, seven days a week running the grocery store.

What's your favorite part of your job?

I like two things about writing. The first is creating new worlds and characters. The other is meeting the children who enjoy those worlds and people that I've created.

What kind of research do you do for your books?

What people don't realize is that the information in a book is only the tip of the iceberg. It requires a lot of reading to get a feel for a time period or an environment, even though I may only use a few facts from what I've gathered. I tell children that when I researched the background to *Dragonwings*, it was a bit like building a house out of toothpicks, and I had to go around the country to find enough toothpicks to use. One recent project involved few sources in English, so I had to hire someone to translate medieval Chinese.

What would you like readers to take away from your books?

I'd like my readers to realize that it's OK to be different. In fact, those very differences can become strengths. It's a question of finding the right context [meaning] for yourself.

Glossary

Asian (AY-zhin) Relating to people from the continent called Asia.

asthma (AZ-muh) A condition that causes difficulty breathing.

athletic (ath-LEH-tik) Having ability and training in sports and exercises of strength.

cable car (KAY-bul KAR) A trainlike car pulled along a railway by a moving cable.

Catholic (KATH-lik) Relating to the Roman Catholic religion.

characters (KAYR-ik-turz) The people or the animals in a story.

Chinatown (CHY-nuh-town) The Chinese section of any city outside China.

cultures (KUL-churz) The beliefs, customs, art, and religions of a group of people.

editor (EH-dih-ter) The person who corrects errors, checks facts, and decides what will be printed in a newspaper, book, or magazine.

fiction (FIK-shun) Stories that tell about people and events that are not real.

heritage (HER-ih-tij) The stories and ways of doing things that are handed down from parent to child.

Hispanic (hih-SPA-nik) Relating to the people, language, and culture of Spain or Latin America.

housing projects (HOW-zing PRAH-jeks) Low-cost housing for low-income families.

journalism (JER-nul-ih-zum) The business of gathering, writing, and presenting news for a newspaper or magazine.

published (PUH-blishd) Printed and sold in a book, magazine, or newspaper.

rebelled (ruh-BELD) Disobeyed or fought against those in charge.

Index

C
Chinatown, 6, 13, 22
Chinese American, 5, 13

D
Dragon's Gate, 21
Dragonwings, 21–22

H
Harper & Row, Publishers, Inc., 18

L
Lee, Franche (mother), 6

M
Marquette University, 17–18

N
Newbery Honor, 21

P
Pirates of Oz, The, 10

R
Ryder, Joanne (wife), 18, 21

S
Saint Ignatius, 14
San Francisco, California, 5–6, 17
"Selchey Kids, The," 17
Sunnyvale, California, 21
Sweetwater, 18

Y
Yep, Thomas "Spike" (brother), 6, 9
Yep Gim Lew (father), 6, 9

Web Sites

Due to the changing nature of Internet links, PowerKids Press has developed an online list of Web sites related to the subject of this book. This site is updated regularly. Please use this link to access the list:

www.powerkidslinks.com/aa/lauryep/